Group Growth Guide

A Ten-Week, Small Group Guide for Awakening the Light

Includes Grounding Exercises, Icebreakers & Exploration Questions

TAMBRY HARRIS

SPARK Publications
Charlotte, North Carolina

Group Growth Guide:
A Ten-Week, Small Group Guide for Awakening the Light
Tambry Harris

Copyright © 2021 by Tambry Harris. All rights reserved. No part of this book may be used or reproduced in any manner whatsoever without written permission from the author, except in the case of brief quotations embodied in critical articles or reviews. For permissions requests, please contact the author at tambry@survivorstothrivers.com.

Designed, produced, and published by SPARK Publications
SPARKpublications.com
Charlotte, North Carolina

Stock images by Unsplash artists Aaron Buren, Erda Estremera, Jan Tinneberg, Omer Salom, Yuichi Kageyama and Zoltan Tasi.

Softcover, May 2021, ISBN: 978-1-953555-12-0

Introduction

Welcome to this opportunity to *Awaken Your Light* and claim your *Going-Forward Story!* This journey is one that takes courage and having a trusted group around you to support this growth can be a helpful step. Because this is deep work and group trust is important, the first week you will spend time getting to know one another a little better and setting "ground rules" that will help you feel safe in this space together.

Purpose

This Group Guide was developed to help survivors of abuse and trauma look at their stories and understand how limiting beliefs may keep them in unhealthy patterns. The author shares her story, her limiting beliefs and her unhealthy patterns to model that they exist for everyone AND you don't have to stay in that space. By working through this Guide, you can examine those things that may be holding you back from a thriving life and your authentic self.

Flow

Each discussion will take around one hour and thirty minutes depending upon how much conversation is generated in the Book Insight and Deeper Exploration time.

Your group can decide on how you want to schedule your meetings. Options include:
- Meeting weekly which will create a natural rhythm and allow immediate processing of exercises completed in the book.
- Monthly meetings allow more time to complete the exercises and do individual processing.
- Bi-monthly (twice a month) could be a happy medium.

A pattern is set for every meeting so that you can ground yourself as a group and walk through the book's reflection exercises in a helpful, exploratory way.

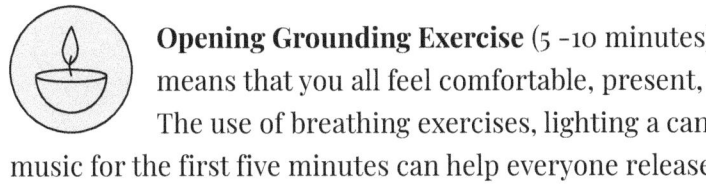

Opening Grounding Exercise (5 -10 minutes) - The word "ground" means that you all feel comfortable, present, and safe in the room. The use of breathing exercises, lighting a candle, and perhaps using music for the first five minutes can help everyone release tension. A different type of breathing exercise is offered each meeting to allow group members to experience new ways of getting centered and learn to build a practice for themselves.

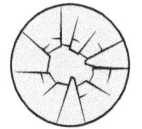

Icebreaker (10 – 15 minutes) – A question is offered to help everyone begin to share a little and find their voice. There is always freedom to share as much or as little as you want at this time. As the group moves through the ten weeks, people gradually increase in their comfort to share.

Book Insights (20 minutes) – Reflections around what was read and responses to the questions are shared. If people highlighted certain things, ask them to share what was meaningful about that sentence or section. The group can also walk through the chapters and talk about what resonated with them, what was encouraging or how it took their understanding of an experience or concept to a deeper level.

Break (5 minutes) - Inserting a break between Book Insights and Deeper Exploration allows the group to have a collective breath. Try to stay in the "grounded" attitude and come back quietly into the safe space. It is best not to have people step away from the group for an individual conversation since the sharing is so deep and personal. This time is meant for a restroom break, to get a drink or to take a couple of minutes to center and listen to your body.

Deeper Exploration (30 minutes) - Questions are offered to go beyond the initial book questions to deepen understanding and have a safe space to explore questions and feelings members of the group might have. If the group goes deep into a question, you may not have time to discuss them all. That is just fine. The purpose is deeper exploration and if one question takes the group into deeper understanding then that is *wonderful*! An option if you do not get to all the questions is that members can capture their thoughts about those questions in their journal between meeting and bring back insights to the next meeting. One thing to note: this is a group discussion and if one person is dominating the time and it feels like a monologue, this needs to be lovingly addressed. Ground rules to manage this will be important.

Support Request (5 minutes) – This group is there to support one another. Each member should have the opportunity to share a specific request they may have as they are on this journey. Some groups may be comfortable naming this as "prayers" and others may just choose to hold the requests in their hearts during their time apart.

Closing (5 minutes) – Similar to the opening exercise, the goal is to have everyone leave feeling "grounded". Everyone should take three deep, cleansing breaths. Next reflect on a thought or intention that they would like to share with the group in closing. Go around the circle and share the thought, word, or phrase. Blow out the candle for a final closing (if lit one).

Setting

The space needs to be one that is welcoming for all. This book was published in a time where social distancing and meetings/gatherings moved to virtual platforms. For both virtual and in-person meetings, it is recommended that the group be kept to seven people or less given the nature of the book and deep discussion.

- If in person, chairs should be set in a circle around a table. A candle in the center of the table allows for a centering point for all. If you wish to "soften" the table further, a cloth could be placed on the table. Lower lighting (vs florescent or strong overhead lighting) will make the room feel more comfortable and will contribute to the grounding effect. Each person may wish to have an accompanying journal to capture additional reflections.
- If the meeting is virtual, establish what platform you will use. Being able to "see" one another will be important because visual cues are helpful in creating safety. Each person will need to establish their "welcoming space" where they can have privacy and feel grounded with their individual candle.

Small-Group Leader

It will be up to the group as to whether you have a designated leader or rotate that role. The main responsibilities are to manage time and ensure everyone adheres to ground rules, although every member should feel the responsibility to hold each other accountable. The leader would be responsible for convening the group and having music if the group decides that is how they would like to "enter" the space. The leader should also be ready to share reflections initially to get the group going and set the tone for the group.

Ground Rules

These are some suggested "ground rules" for your group. Discuss them in your first meeting, adapt them so that they feel like yours and add ones that will be helpful for the group.

- Share what you are comfortable sharing. This is a deep topic, and no one should feel they must reveal anything of which they are uncomfortable.
- The group is not here to "fix" a person or a situation. Problems and challenges will be shared. Because everyone is entering with a tender and understanding heart, there is a tendency to find solutions. It is the group's role to hold space for the individual to find their truth and their answers.
- Allow room for silence, and even tears. Vulnerability is essential in this work. Often, we need silence and space to find our thoughts and voices. As survivors, we have had to be tough but as the book walks you through healing steps, you will have to be open to your woundedness. That may lead to tears which are a helpful release of the pent-up pain.
- At the same time, it will be important for you to manage yourself. If you notice that the focus often shifts from the group to supporting you, check yourself. If you find yourself needing additional support, it may be a good idea to engage a therapist to help provide the needed counseling.
- Speak only for yourself about beliefs, feelings, and responses.
- Respect and receive what others offer graciously to maintain safety.
- Maintain confidentiality. There is a concept called "double confidentiality," which means not only do you not repeat anything that is shared within the group but also you don't bring it up with the individual who shared outside of the group unless they do.
- Determine your expectations around attendance. Given the nature of the conversation and the way the book builds on experience, it is helpful for everyone to be present at every meeting. Of course, situations arise but efforts should be made to commit to this groups and the time together.

Resources

- The organization, Going Forward: Survivors to Thrivers is a resource to you as you move through the book. Survivorstothrivers.com
- We have a bi-monthly blog which provides thought-provoking perspectives and self-care exercises. Survivorstothrivers.com/blog
- Our Instagram and Facebook posts offer encouragement throughout the week with motivational quotes and highlights of survivors moving to thriving and finding their voices. Our Twitter is used to share exciting information. Instagram – survivorstothrivers, Facebook – survivorstothriversofficial, and Twitter – survivorstothrivers@GFS2T
- If you decide you would like a certified facilitator to lead the group, contact us through the website.

SESSION 1

Group Formation

OPENING GROUNDING EXERCISE
10 Minutes
The word "ground" means that you all feel comfortable, present, and safe in the room.

- Ways to ground the group include breathing exercises, lighting a candle, and perhaps using music for the first five minutes to help everyone release tension.
- Spend more time on this for the first session so everyone understands the importance of this exercise.
- Try this for your opening meeting:
  - Light the candle stating, "We light this candle to illuminate this sacred space of growth and the space within ourselves as we seek to Awaken our Light together."
  - "As we enter this time together, let's get grounded by having our feet firmly planted on the ground. You can close your eyes if this is comfortable for you or you can gaze gently at the candle."
  - "Now take three deep, cleansing breaths. Notice your body settling into your chair with each breath."
  - Say, "We are going to go through a breathing 'visualization' exercise where I invite you to 'breathe' calmness into your body. We will start with the forehead – take a breath and notice any tension you may have in that space. Breathe in calm and breathe out any tension. Slowly do this 'body scan' as you move down to chin, shoulders, chest, hips, legs and feet."
  - "Now, we will end with natural breathing and noticing the easy flow through our bodies."
- Let them know that when they are ready, they can gently open their eyes.

GUIDELINES FOR MEETINGS
15 Minutes
Discuss format of guided sessions and "ground rules"

- **Outline Flow of Sessions** - Share that you will work on two chapters between each session (with the exception of Week 7). Mention that having an additional journal or notebook may be helpful to capture thoughts from the discussion.

12 | Awakening the Light

- **Agree upon "Leader Role"** - Will the role of Leader be one person or rotated? If it will be a rotated role, go ahead and have members volunteer to lead certain sessions so this piece of business is addressed and so people can know when their week to lead will be. Capture contact information to be able to communicate with one another between sessions.
- **Share Suggested Ground Rules** and see what modifications people would like (full ground rules detail can be found in the Introduction). Add additional ground rules that would be helpful for the group. Gain final agreement on ground rules. Determine who will capture them and share final version with the group.
    - Share what you are comfortable sharing.
    - The group is not here to "fix" a person or a situation.
    - Allow room for silence, and even tears. Vulnerability is essential in this work.
    - Manage yourself and notice if the focus is on supporting just you.
    - Speak only for yourself about beliefs, feelings, and responses.
    - Respect and receive what others offer graciously to maintain safety.
    - Maintain confidentiality and double-confidentiality.
    - Determine your expectations around attendance.
    - Add other ground rules.

GROUP EXPLORATION
45 Minutes
Get to know one another better and build trust

- Depending on how well the group knows one another, basic introductions may be needed such as: What is your name? How did you find out about the study? What part of town do you live in?
- What interested you about this study?
- What do you hope to get out of this study?
- What are you nervous about as you enter these next 9 weeks?
- Knowing the others in the group, is there anything you would like to ask for support as you enter this growth experience together?

CLOSING
5 Minutes

- Similar to the opening exercise, the goal is to have everyone leave feeling "grounded".
- Everyone should take three deep, cleansing breaths.
- Next reflect on a thought or intention that would like to share with the group in closing. Go around the circle and share the thought, word, or phrase.
- Blow out the candle for a final closing.

FOR OUR NEXT TIME TOGETHER
Chapters 1 & 2: Framing & Forming
Complete reading and exercises

SESSION 2

Chapters 1 & 2: Framing and Forming

OPENING GROUNDING EXERCISE
5 Minutes

- Light a candle in the center of the table for a focal point.
- Invite everyone to take three slow, deep cleansing breaths.
- Ask everyone to do a "body scan" reminding them of what this is (walking down through the body to notice any tension and release it).
- Ask them to breathe in whatever is helpful to them and breathe out anything that is not helpful or encouraging of growth.
- Sometimes it is helpful to have a word that you breathe in and out. A word that you breathe in could be "calm", "peace", "love", "be" and a word to breathe out could be "fear", "stress", "anxiety", etc.
- Now breathe easily in and out as you seek to release any tension from the day.
- Playing a song or music to help center can also be helpful.

ICE BREAKER
15 Minutes

- What did you think when you read the quote: "With each raised voice and each healed heart, we begin to change the culture that silences innocent victims. We stop the shame, secrecy, and silence and promote hope, healing, and health?"
- Had you heard about the study that linked ACEs with illnesses? Does that help motivate you to do the healing? How?

BOOK INSIGHTS
20 Minutes
Reflections around what was read and responses to the questions are offered

- Often survivors find themselves living in their heads not even "feeling" their bodies; what is your sense of this for yourself?

- What healing do you want or need to do? (share at whatever level is comfortable for you)
- Can you begin to name fears that may get in the way of the healing? (By naming them, we take away their power)
- Are there any messages that you recognize became ingrained in you from childhood?
- Is there anything you would like to share as you captured your thoughts around family dynamics and childhood memories?

BREAK
5 Minutes

- Inserting a break between Book Insights and Deeper Exploration allows the group to have a collective breath.
- Try to stay in the "grounded" attitude and come back quietly into the safe space.
- It is best not to have people step away from the group for an individual conversation since the sharing is so deep and personal.
- Use this time for a restroom break, to get a drink, or to take a couple of minutes to breathe and center yourself to listen to your body.

DEEPER EXPLORATION
30 Minutes

Questions are offered to go beyond the initial book questions to expand and deepen understanding

- As we reenter the room, let's take three deep breaths again to center ourselves. As you do that, is there anything you notice about your body? Do you feel any tension or anxiety?
- What work have you done in the past to be mindful of your body? What has been helpful?
- What was it like to begin to think about the stories that define you?
- Did the "corner pieces" concept resonate? Where do you feel like you are on your puzzle?

SUPPORT REQUEST AND CLOSING
10 Minutes

- Since the group is beginning to define how it operates, check in to see how well ground rules were followed. Is there something to pay attention to next time?
- This group is there to support one another. Each member should have the opportunity to share a specific request they may have as they are on this journey.
- Similar to the opening exercise, the goal is to have everyone leave feeling "grounded". Everyone should take three deep, cleansing breaths. Next reflect on a thought or intention that would like to share with the group in closing. Go around the circle and share the thought, word, or phrase. Blow out the candle for a final closing.

> Like a butterfly coming out of her cocoon, my wings were spreading and my beauty beginning to come forth.
>
> Tambry Harris

SESSION 3

Chapters 3 & 4: Launching and Evolving

OPENING GROUNDING EXERCISE
10 Minutes

- Light a candle in the center of the table for a focal point.
- Invite everyone to take three slow, deep cleansing breaths.
- Introduce the concept of "belly breathing" which is officially called "Diaphragmatic breathing". Many people get into the habit of breathing only with their chests. Restrictive clothing, poor posture, stress, and conditions that weaken the muscles involved in breathing ALL contribute to chest breathing.
    - Sit comfortably in your chair with your feet flat on the ground. Your knees should be bent and your head, neck, and shoulders, relaxed. Although you don't need to sit straight as an arrow, you also don't want to slouch.
    - Place one hand on your upper chest. This hand should remain relatively still (compared to the hand you'll place on your belly) as you breathe in and out.
    - The other hand should be placed below your ribcage and right above your navel. Having a hand here will allow you to feel your diaphragm move as you breathe.
    - Breathe in slowly through your nose. The air going into your nose should move downward so that you feel your stomach rise with your other hand. Don't force or push your abdominal muscles outward.
    - The movement (and the airflow) should be smooth. You shouldn't feel like you're forcing your lower belly out by clenching your muscles.
    - The hand on your chest should remain relatively still.
    - Let your belly relax. You should feel the hand that's over it fall inward (toward your spine). Don't force your stomach inward by squeezing or clenching your muscles.
    - Exhale slowly through slightly pursed lips. The hand on your chest should continue to remain relatively still.
    - If you feel lightheaded at any time, discontinue the breathing exercise.
    - Notice how you feel after going through this breathing exercise.
- As we close, breathe in whatever is helpful to you and breathe out anything that is not. Seek to release any tension from the day.

ICE BREAKER
10 Minutes

- What did you think when you read the quote: "I believe many women have had their lives altered by abuse"?
- What do you think contributes to the various aspects of a person's personality?

BOOK INSIGHTS
20 Minutes

- When the author spoke of circumstances where she wanted to take action but found herself stuck, what did you think? Could you relate? How?
- What gives you the strength to take action?
- Is there anything you would like to share about unhealthy relationships or situations you found yourself in and what support you needed?
- Thinking about Exercises 15 and 16, what do you want to begin to claim for yourself?

BREAK
5 Minutes

- Encourage the group to have a collective breath.
- Use this time for whatever you need – restroom break, getting water, checking in with yourself using breath and silence.
- Try to stay in the "grounded" attitude and come back quietly into the safe space.

DEEPER EXPLORATION
30 Minutes

- What does the word "vulnerability" mean to you? What helps you to be vulnerable?
- What do you find getting in the way of living your authentic life/embracing your whole self?
- If you were to describe your authentic self/how you want to be seen, what does that look like?
- The metaphor of a stream creating a ravine was offered in the book. Does that speak to you? Or is there another image you would offer around our ingrained patterns?
- Do you agree or disagree with, "I also realized that if you live life avoiding risks, you will experience nothing, impact no one and have little meaning in life"? Why or why not.

SUPPORT REQUEST AND CLOSING
10 Minutes

- Support Request - Each member should have the opportunity to share a specific request they may have on this journey.
- Closing - Everyone should take three deep, cleansing breaths. Next reflect on a thought or intention that could be shared with the group in closing. Go around the circle and share the thought, word, or phrase. Blow out the candle for a final closing.

> "I wanted to embrace this new direction and show more of me. Yet I felt deeply that being real and vulnerable was not safe.
>
> Tambry Harris"

SESSION 4

Chapters 5 & 6: Awakening and Claiming

OPENING GROUNDING EXERCISE
10 Minutes

- Light a candle in the center of the table for a focal point.
- Invite everyone to take three slow, deep cleansing breaths.
- Introduce Box Breathing which is also known as four-square breathing. Box breathing can reduce stress and improve your mood. It can also help treat insomnia by allowing you to calm your nervous system at night before bed. Box breathing can even help with pain management. It is a technique used by taking slow, deep breaths.
- To start, make sure that you're seated upright in a comfortable chair with your feet flat on the floor. Keeping your hands relaxed in your lap with your palms facing up, focus on your posture. You should be sitting up straight. This will help you take deep breaths.
- Step 1: Slowly exhale through your mouth, getting all the oxygen out of your lungs. Focus on this intention and be conscious of what you're doing.
- Step 2: Inhale slowly and deeply through your nose to the count of four. In this step, count to four very slowly in your head. Feel the air fill your lungs, one section at a time, until your lungs are completely full and the air moves into your abdomen.
- Step 3: Hold your breath for another slow count of four.
- Step 4: Exhale through your mouth for the same slow count of four, expelling the air from your lungs and abdomen. Be conscious of the feeling of air leaving your lungs.
- Step 5: Hold your breath for the same slow count of four before repeating this process.

ICE BREAKER
15 Minutes

- As you have been working through this book, imagine you are a fish who is swimming in water. Tell me about the water. Is it murky? Is it becoming increasingly clear? What are you noticing?

- Another way to ask this is, "Are you beginning to see and notice things that have escaped you previously? As you notice these new things, how are you taking in this new awareness?"

BOOK INSIGHTS
20 Minutes

- What growth metaphors from the book spoke to you? Is there another one you think would be even more accurate, more helpful? Please share.
- Would anyone like to share what they captured in Exercise 21, what they would like to claim? Own? Release?
- If it is easier, share what rocks they would like to release from Exercise 22?
- The exercises in Chapter 6 are deep and personal. This group is here to process learnings and awareness, please share what you would like to explore from Exercise 24 – 27.

BREAK
5 Minutes

- Inserting a break between Book Insights and Deeper Exploration allows the group to have a collective breath.
- Try to stay in the "grounded" attitude and come back quietly into the safe space.

DEEPER EXPLORATION
30 Minutes

- To what degree have you been in touch with your body?
- We have had "support requests" in our previous meetings but as we move through the book, the importance of this grows. How is your awareness around what you need in the way of support increasing?

- Be quiet and still for a couple of minutes. Let's take time to listen to our bodies. Breathe in three deep, belly breaths. Pay attention to see what you notice.
- Did you hear anything new? What is your body asking for or telling you? How can this group support you?

SUPPORT REQUEST AND CLOSING
10 Minutes

- Support needs were deeply discussed. Provide one last opportunity to share a specific request they may have on this journey.
- Similar to the opening exercise, the goal is to have everyone leave feeling "grounded". Everyone should take three deep, cleansing breaths. Next reflect on a thought or intention that could be shared with the group. Go around the circle and share the thought, word, or phrase. Blow out the candle for a final closing.

> "My inner knowing told me I needed to move through many layers before I could be free."

SESSION 5

Chapters 7 & 8: Thriving and Encouraging Thriving

OPENING GROUNDING EXERCISE
5 Minutes

- Light a candle in the center of the table for a focal point.
- Invite everyone to take three slow, deep cleansing breaths. Notice your body settling into your chair with each breath.
- We are going to do the breathing "visualization" exercise where I invite you to "breathe" calmness into your body.
    - We will start with the forehead – take a breath and notice any tension you may have in that space.
    - Breathe in calm and breathe out any tension.
    - Slowly do this "body scan" as you move down to chin, shoulders, chest, hips, legs, and feet.
- End with natural breathing and noticing the easy flow through your body.

ICE BREAKER
15 Minutes

- Ask if anyone has heard of "neuroplasticity" or "neural pathways". Have them share what they know.
- Build on what was shared: neuroplasticity is the brain's ability to learn and adapt. Until relatively recently, experts believed that our brains were fixed by the end of adolescence and that, in terms of neurons, it was all downhill from there. But the latest research has proved quite the opposite. Our brains can actually grow and change throughout adulthood.
- "The main point of neuroplasticity is that you can actually form and reorganize connections in your brain," says Dr. Marsha Chinichian, a Los Angeles-based clinical psychotherapist and the brains behind the acclaimed mental fitness app, Mindshine. "For a long time we thought that humans were born with a ton of neurons, synapses, and connections, and as we got older, they simply died off. But now we've learned that isn't true. We can actually make changes to further develop our brains. We've learned we can actually rewire our brains."

- There are a number of ways to build neuroplasticity including what you eat and exercise. It has also been shown that using your non-dominant hand to do simple tasks such as brushing your teeth, texting, or stirring your coffee/tea can help you form new neural pathways. These cognitive exercises, also known as "neurobics," strengthen connectivity between your brain cells. "It's like having more cell towers in your brain to send messages along. The more cell towers you have, the fewer missed calls," explains Dr. P. Murali Doraiswamy, chief of biological psychiatry at Duke University Medical Center.
- Here is an exercise to try. Everyone write their name with their non-dominant hand. Rewrite it 10 times with that hand and notice if it gets easier.
- Share your experience with each other. How might this apply as we seek to thrive in our daily lives and break unhealthy patterns?

BOOK INSIGHTS
20 Minutes

- Are there patterns or routines you might be creating as you move through the book and the exercises? What are you learning about yourself?
- Did the concept of our life being a mosaic speak to you? Do you have a sense of what your mosaic looks like right now? Can you describe it for others? What pieces are being added?
- What would you like to share from either Exercise 33 or 34?
- What can you share about your response to the questions around fear (in Exercise 35)? What would be helpful to name? To tame?

BREAK
5 Minutes

- Inserting a break between Book Insights and Deeper Exploration allows the group to have a collective breath.

- Try to stay in the "grounded" attitude and come back quietly into the safe space.

DEEPER EXPLORATION
30 Minutes

- How were you affected when the #metoo voices started coming out in 2017?
- How does doing this work address those feelings?
- How does this group help you feel strength to claim your going forward chapter?

SUPPORT REQUEST AND CLOSING
10 Minutes

- We have just completed Section I of the book. Now is a good time to check in to see how you are supporting one another. Are you adhering to the Ground Rules? Is there anything that needs to be changed with the structure of your time together?
- This group is here to support one another. Each member should have the opportunity to share a specific request they may have on this part of the journey.
- Similar to the opening exercise, the goal is to have everyone leave feeling "grounded". Everyone should take three deep, cleansing breaths. Next, reflect on a thought or intention that they would like to share with the group in closing. Go around the circle and share the thought, word, or phrase. Blow out the candle for a final closing.

For Next Time Complete Chapters 9 & 10

> "I had lived in a dark and limiting box, familiar and safe. This self-imposed box hindered my growth, my experiences, and my exposure. I knew it was time to leave the box to begin thriving."
>
> — Tambry Harris

SECTION II

Your Going-Forward Story

SESSION 6

Chapters 9 & 10: Welcoming Change and Honoring Self

OPENING GROUNDING EXERCISE
5 Minutes

- Light a candle in the center of the table for a focal point. Welcome everyone to the space.
- "Now that we are in our sixth session, it is becoming clear that our breath is the key to being grounded as well as to a calm and steady heart rhythm. We also know it is not just any breath. It is intentional. It is slow."
- Let's try another type of breathing exercise.
    - Take a long exhale.
    - Breath in for a count of four.
    - Hold for a count of two.
    - Exhale for a count of eight.
    - Pause for a count of two.
    - Repeat.
- Ask what they noticed about this type of breathing.
- Share that this type of breathing stimulates the vagus nerve. Here are some links if you would like to learn more:
    - https://www.thecut.com/2019/05/i-now-suspect-the-vagus-nerve-is-the-key-to-well-being.html
    - https://medium.com/mind-cafe/how-to-stimulate-your-vagus-nerve-and-decompress-with-a-4-8-breathing-technique-d1ca7ff6be25

ICE BREAKER
15 Minutes

- Have you ever heard of Maslow's Hierarchy of Needs? What do you remember about it?
- Build upon what is shared with information from the diagram on the next page.
- What is your sense of "self-actualization"?
- Have you seen it achieved? What did it look like?

Self-actualization
desire to become the most that one can be

Esteem
respect, self-esteem, status, recognition, strength, freedom

Love and belonging
friendship, intimacy, family, sense of connection

Safety needs
personal security, employment, resources, health, property

Physiological needs
air, water, food, shelter, sleep, clothing, reproduction

BOOK INSIGHTS
20 Minutes

- Do you relate to the transformational process of refining gold or creating a sculpture? Do you have a better metaphor to share?
- What would you like to share about the "door of your heart" from Exercise 37?
- What are your thoughts about shifting from your current chapter to a new one?

BREAK
5 Minutes

- Use break for a collective breath.
- When the group is back together, walk them through a "body scan" starting with the forehead, then the brow, mouth, shoulders and slowly down to feet.
  - What do they notice?
  - What is their experience listening to their body? Is this new for them?

DEEPER EXPLORATION
30 Minutes

- Why do you think a whole chapter is focused on change?
- How do you typically move through change?
- What do you need to be intentional about as you let go of this chapter to embrace the next?

SUPPORT REQUEST AND CLOSING
10 Minutes

- Is there something the group can do to support you and encourage you as you embrace change? As you seek to embrace the whole of you?
- Tell the group that the next chapter will involve a deeper dive and incorporate more reflection. When we come together next, they can share as much or as little as they want.
- To feel "grounded", everyone take three deep, cleansing breaths.
- Next reflect on a thought or intention that you would like to share with the group in closing. Go around the circle and share the thought, word, or phrase.
- Blow out the candle for a final closing.

For Next Session – Read and Do Exercises for Only
Chapter 11: Examining the Core of You

> We have to 'unfreeze' ourselves from the protective layers that have been formed in order to get to the real, core part of ourselves.
>
> Tambry Harris

SESSION 7

Chapter 11:
Examining the Core of You

OPENING GROUNDING EXERCISE
5 Minutes

- Light a candle in the center of the table for a focal point.
- Welcome everyone to the space and remind them that they should feel comfortable sharing as much or as little as they want.
- Invite everyone to take three slow, deep cleansing breaths.
- As you inhale, breathe in what you need or want to claim for yourself.
- As you exhale, breathe out that which is not helpful or useful.
- Repeat three times.

ICE BREAKER
15 Minutes

- The book encourages you to look at yourself as the main character of the story. How was that for you?
- Why do you think you were asked to look at yourself and your story from that lens?

BOOK INSIGHTS
20 Minutes

- What would you like to share from your character sketch (Exercises 45 – 47)?
- How did you define mind, body, and spirit?
- After everyone has had a chance to share, how does hearing other definitions expand yours?
- What is your sense of limiting core beliefs?
- Do you have an example of how beliefs can impact thoughts that then impact behaviors?
- Do you believe that we can shift those core beliefs from positive to negative? Why or why not? (if the group does not believe that they can be shifted, remind them about neuroplasticity)

BREAK
5 Minutes

- Use this time for a restroom break, to get a drink, or to take a couple of minutes to breath and center yourself. Listen to your body.
- When everyone returns from the break, re-ground using the breathing technique from earlier.
  - Breathe in what you need.
  - Breathe out that which is not helpful.

DEEPER EXPLORATION
30 Minutes

Framing for this Deeper Exploration time is important as you are getting into the depth of people's story. It is important that they feel safe and supported during this time.
- Begin by stating: "This is where having a group growing and exploring together is helpful. A group of kindred spirits to support you as you look at the 'hard stuff' is invaluable."
- "You have been building trust with one another over the past six weeks. As I mentioned before, share whatever is helpful to you as you navigate your path forward."

Move into the deeper exploration questions. Explore what each person shares to allow depth of understanding.
- What have you learned about your limiting belief(s)?
- What strengths or points of light do you want to highlight or claim?

SUPPORT REQUEST AND CLOSING
10 Minutes

- In Exercise 58, you identified a healing prayer of intention. Would you like to share it with the others?
- Are there other support requests anyone has?
- Given the depth of sharing, it is important for everyone leave feeling "grounded". Everyone should take three deep, cleansing breaths. Next reflect on a thought or intention that they would like to share with the group in closing. Go around the circle and share the thought, word, or phrase.
- Blow out the candle for a final closing.

Emma Mansfield, a young artist and survivor from Pembroke, NC created this beautiful piece of art with a quote from the book, Awakening the Light. If you are interested in purchasing a print, contact us at survivorstothrivers.com

We are all wounded in some way. What we do with our woundedness defines us. If we learn & grow from our wounds, they can motivate us to claim our Going-Forward Story.

—TAMBRY HARRIS

SESSION 8

Chapters 12 &13: Embracing Mindfulness and Describing Desired Self

OPENING GROUNDING EXERCISE
5 Minutes

- Light a candle in the center of the table for a focal point. Invite everyone into this sacred space.
- Remind them of the mindfulness practice they did in Exercise 61. It was one where they practiced "cleansing breaths" for five minutes by themselves.
- Open with a minute of cleansing breaths. Breathe slowly and deeply for a count of five. Feel the air expand your lungs and your stomach. Then release your breath slowly for a count of five. As you do this, notice where you feel tension and if it is released.
- Ask if anyone would like to share how it was to practice the cleansing breaths on their own or what they noticed in their bodies.

ICE BREAKER
15 Minutes

- What is your understanding of "mindfulness"?
- Do you have any current practices? What are they?
- Talk about the various kinds of mindfulness practices. These practices offer you an opportunity to slow down and allow yourself to be present to all that is around and within you. If they need help coming up with some, you can mention:
    - Mindful eating (savor eat bit, notice the flavor and texture of food, chew slowly and notice when you swallow, pause before next bite).
    - Mindful walking (walk in silence noticing the sounds around you, walk with heel of foot first rolling to the ball of your foot, notice your breath as you walk, the wind as it touches your skin).
    - Mindful meditating (is your body relaxed, where is tension, how deep is your breath, can you notice the pace of your breathing, what sounds are around you, can you let distractions including thoughts flow in and out of your awareness to stay focused).

BOOK INSIGHTS
20 Minutes

- What do you want to claim for yourself (from Exercise 62)?
- Are there elements of your outer or inner story you would like to share?
- What is your Going-Forward Chapter name? *(as people are sharing their Going-Forward Chapter Names, capture them on a piece of paper so you can read them back to celebrate them once all are collected)*

BREAK
5 Minutes

- Use this time for a restroom break, to get a drink, or to take a couple of minutes to breath and center yourself to listen to your body.

DEEPER EXPLORATION
30 Minutes

- What was it like to rewrite your story and current chapter incorporating mood and tone given what you want to emphasize?
- Is there anything of your summary you want to share or explore with others? *This is a time to begin to voice your desired Going-Forward Chapter!*

SUPPORT REQUEST AND CLOSING
10 Minutes

- Is there support you need as you seek to engage others or incorporate specific practices?
- Reflect on a thought or intention that they would like to share with the group in closing. Go around the circle and share the thought, word, or phrase. Blow out the candle for a final closing.

> "It is now your turn to walk confidently through the door into your next chapter!
>
> Tambry Harris"

SESSION 9

Chapters 14 & 15: Claiming Going-Forward Story and Growing

OPENING GROUNDING EXERCISE
10 Minutes

- Light a candle in the center of the table for a focal point. Welcome everyone into the space.
- Today we are going to focus on self-care as well as mindfulness. As we become more in tune with our bodies, we become more aware of the need to take care of ourselves and release tension that our bodies may hold. Below are self-care exercises for our hands and feet. Take time to walk through each so everyone has a chance to practice lovingly massaging these areas.

HANDS
Start by rubbing all the fingers of your left hand with your right, moving in a circular motion from the base of the finger to the tip, focusing on the joints. Then, gently pull each finger away from the hand, sliding your grip up from the base of each finger to the tip.
Next, give your palm a massage with your thumb on the palm and your fingers on the back of the hand. In a circular motion, rub the pads of your fingers, the fleshy part between your thumb and wrist, and any other tense or tender points. Switch hands.

FEET
Place your right foot on top of your left thigh. Using both hands, rotate your foot at the ankle. Place one hand on top of your foot and the other on your sole. Rub your hands back and forth across your foot in short strokes. Tailor your self-massage to your needs by using brisk strokes to stimulate (especially helpful for cold feet) or gentle strokes to soothe. Concentrating on the entire foot, toe to heel. With one hand, gently stretch your toes back. With the other hand, use a loose fist or an open palm and gently massage the sole of your foot. Complete your self-massage with long, slow strokes over the entire foot. Then, repeat the sequence on the opposite foot.
What other parts of your body might feel good to rub or stretch? Your shoulders and arms? Your neck? Scalp? Take a couple of minutes to give those parts of your body some love.

ICE BREAKER
10 Minutes

- How does your body feel?
- What sensations do you notice?
- What other kinds of self-care can you suggest for the group? What have you found to be helpful?

BOOK INSIGHTS
20 Minutes

- What obstacles or challenges might get in the way of you living into your Going-Forward story? (Exercise 73)
- How do you plan on addressing these things?
- What changing patterns can you celebrate with this group? (Exercise 75)

BREAK
5 Minutes

- Try to stay in the "grounded" attitude and come back quietly into the safe space.
- Use this time for a restroom break, to get a drink, or to take a couple of minutes to breathe and center yourself to listen to your body.

DEEPER EXPLORATION
30 Minutes

- Earlier in the book the concept of change management was shared. Specifically, a process of "unfreeze – change or move – refreeze" was

described. "Refreezing" means that you intentionally put things in place to help you maintain the new state.
- What steps will be important for you to put in place to help you continue on your path with your Going-Forward Story? Spend a good bit of time exploring ideas as they build on one another.
- In the next session, we will create an illustration to keep in front of us to inspire us and to solidify our Going-Forward Story. Do Not Worry! No art-ability is required. We will create a collage of images to represent our next Chapter.
  - For the next session, we will need pieces of cardboard (the back of a writing pad works great), scissors, glue sticks, index cards and magazines with colorful pictures.
    - If the group is meeting together, everyone bringing a few magazines will provide plenty of options.
    - If the group is meeting virtually, collect what magazines you can, and we will also share some computer resources for pictures you can use.
- Further instructions on how to complete the illustration will be provided when we come back together. Here are some pictures to give you a sense of what this could look like:

SUPPORT REQUEST AND CLOSING
10 Minutes

- We have come a long way on this journey of self-exploration and growth. How can the group continue to support you as you claim your Going-Forward Story?
- Take three deep breaths and reflect on a thought or intention that they would like to share with the group in closing. Go around the circle and share the thought, word, or phrase. Blow out the candle for a final closing.

SESSION 10

Bonus Week Illustrating Your Going-Forward Story

OPENING GROUNDING EXERCISE
10 Minutes

- Light a candle in the center of the table for a focal point. Welcome everyone into the space.
- Invite everyone to take three slow, deep cleansing breaths. Ask them to settle into their seats for a visualization exercise.
- Think about the Going-Forward story you are seeking to claim. See yourself walking into that new chapter. Let them sit in this for a couple of minutes.
    - What do you see?
    - Sense?
    - Feel?
- Imagine what words, images, or colors that come to your mind to reflect what you are experiencing with your senses.
- Feel free to capture these words, images, and colors as they come to you (jot down on piece of paper).
- Close with a breath of gratitude for where this journey has taken you.

ILLUSTRATING YOUR STORY
40 Minutes
Opportunity to make a collage of images and words that capture the next chapters of your Going-Forward Story

Provide an overview of the activity and then walk everyone through the steps. Let them know that a break is incorporated into this time.

For 25 - 30 minutes (this is when they can take an individual break when needed):

- Now it is time to get creative! Think about the words, images and colors that came to mind in our opening exercise. As you look through magazines, notice pictures that speak to you and capture your vision and cut them out. At times images almost jump off the page at you... these are the ones you want. There may be words that speak to you and feel free to cut them out as well. Keep in mind, you want to rely more on pictures as they have even more meaning.

- If you don't have magazines, you can use unsplash.com or pixabay.com for free images that you can copy and print at whatever size you wish. You can also create words with fun fonts and colors in a document and then add pictures that you have found from the free images.

For 10 minutes:
- As you look at the images you found, see how they "come together". Allow your inner wisdom to see how the images come together in unique ways. You may choose to cut them out a little more and overlap some of the images.
- Maybe the images are arranged to represent steps you have or are taking. As you assemble, you can go vertically or horizontally, whatever makes sense to you.
- Maybe you have words mixed with the images.
- Next collage these pieces by gluing them to the cardboard.
- The last step is to glue an index card to the back of the board. **Write on the card what you wish to claim for yourself as you Awaken Your Light and move into your Going-Forward Story:**
  - I am one who... (this statement comes from the message that evolved from your collection of images)
  - My Light is awakening by....
  - My Going-Forward Vision is...

SHARING YOUR ILLUSTRATION
30 Minutes

- Give each person 3-5 minutes to share:
  - What the process of illustrating their Going-Forward Story was like.
  - Why they chose the particular images they chose, how does it illustrate their story?
  - What they wrote on their index card.

FINAL SUPPORT REQUEST AND CLOSING
10 Minutes

- Encourage everyone to put this Going-Forward Story Illustration where they can see it and be inspired.
- This group has supported one another along a deep and vulnerable exploration. We have built a support community of seekers and thrivers. Talk about how you can support one another as you move into your next chapters.
- Remind them of the resources provided by Going Forward: Survivors to Thrivers.
    - At survivorstothrivers.com/resources there is information about Yoga, Yoga Therapy, NIA, Mindfulness and Meditation to help you continue to develop self-care practices.
    - Our Social Media is meant to keep encouraging this community, our Tribe, and we would love for you to follow us. Facebook – survivorstothriversofficial and Instagram – survivorstothrivers.
    - We have a quarterly newsletter to provide encouragement as well as to let you know exciting events we have planned. Contact us to be on our mailing list.
    - There is also a blog twice a month to bring encouragement and ideas for self-care. The Illustration Exercise you went through was shared in our April 15, 2021 blog. We also offer ideas around self-care like our opening exercise of hand and foot massage.
- As we close, everyone take three deep, cleansing breaths. Next, reflect on your thankfulness and gratitude for how you are moving towards your fullest self. We will share this with the group in closing.
- Go around the circle and share whatever is on your heart.
- Blow out the candle for a final closing. As the smoke circles outward, remind them of the spirit that also encircles this group and will move forward with them as they courageously Go Forward.

"
We are never done
with our growth, and
that is actually good.
We can always write
more chapters. God
continues to surprise
me with what my
story is becoming;
it is much bigger
than I ever thought it
could be.

Tambry Harris

"

About the Author

Tambry Harris is a leadership and life coach, survivor of childhood sexual abuse, and founder of **Going Forward: Survivors to Thrivers**, an organization that provides individual guidance, retreats, and speaking engagements to bring awareness and light into the shame, silence, and darkness that surrounds sexual abuse. Tambry has a master's degree in applied psychology and certifications in leadership coaching, spiritual direction, diversity, and change management.

After spending sixteen years in corporate America, Tambry created her own coaching practice to help individuals enhance their effectiveness and claim lives of significance. She found her voice, named her truth, and created a vision around how she could help others who have experienced the pain and shame of sexual abuse to find healing, strength, and freedom. Through her book, *Awakening the Light*, she shares her inspiring journey of moving from survivor to thriver and creating the Going Forward movement. Her dream is that survivors of sexual abuse will no longer be trapped by fear and limitations from their old stories and can claim whole-hearted, life-giving, going-forward stories.

She married the love of her life, Randy, in 2017 and has a daughter from a previous marriage and two stepsons.

Fun Fast Facts
- **Favorite vacation:** anywhere in the mountains or by the coast
- **Hometown:** the Queen City (Charlotte, North Carolina)
- **Favorite exercise:** cardio dance, yoga, and long hikes to beautiful waterfalls
- **Dream home:** on the water facing west for sunsets
- **Favorite 1980s band:** Journey

🌐 survivorstothrivers.com
✉ tambry@survivorstothrivers.com
f survivorstothriversofficial
⊙ survivorstothrivers
🐦 GFS2T

Going Forward
Survivors to Thrivers

www.ingramcontent.com/pod-product-compliance
Lightning Source LLC
Chambersburg PA
CBHW082041080526
44578CB00009B/802